A Fat Girl's Confidence

I'm Fat. So What?

Patrice Shavone Brown

ISBN-13: 978-1-7328818-2-2

My Story Publishing

Table of Contents

Introduction

I am Patrice Shavone Brown, a Mental Health Counselor, and Director. I am an author, motivational speaker, life coach, actress, and a single mother. I own a mental health facility, which I have run for five years at the time of this writing. I am the oldest of three siblings and have a disability, which motivated me into a helpers' profession.

I have struggled with my weight for years to the point that the ups and downs of gaining weight are no longer something I would be ashamed of. I have learned that I have to love myself regardless of my size. This was never easy for me because I had certain family members who would say, "You are getting bigger; you need to stop eating." "Now stop eating!" Yes, people said mean things to me and, trust me, they stung me like bees. You see, in my journey of being a fat girl, I found peace and acceptance of myself first. Before my confidence began, I had to develop strength.

Although what I am about to share may seem crazy, it is not. When building on anything in life, you have to practice and strengthen yourself. You have to admit that you are fat and prepare your mind for people's reactions. This preparation gets you ready to respond to the judgments of others. Confidence begins when you have prepared yourself and accepted your flaws. Self-esteem building is all about knowing that you are important, needed, loved, and different, and that we all have flaws but are beautiful still.

I have written this book, A Fat Girl's Confidence, so that you can become aware of my journey into the recognition of myself as beautiful; fat or big notwithstanding. As a woman shaped differently (by society's standard for beauty), I have been challenged to write about my feelings and experiences as I was labeled obese at the age of 30.

The word obese seems harsh but funny to me. I had always heard fat and was okay with being just fat. Obese sounds like I am a big, fat case of death monster! Say it, O-BEE-S. So now, society has labeled me a beast because I am fat. If the word obesity is not enough to kill one's self-esteem or confidence, I do not know what will. I am motivated to share my tips of confidence because, even with the label obese, I still love what I see in the mirror.

As a teenager, boys loved me and, yes, in school boys crushed on fat girls too. As an adult, men like me for what they see in me. I don't want any female that is a size 8 or below to make you feel like you are a nobody just because you are fat. If you are a teenager or a grown woman battling with weight and negative comments from others, hold on beautiful, your motivational fat girl is here to help you feel better about being you!

I have come to inspire you into a one-week commitment to change your mindset about being fat. My mindset is that I am always going to be fat or big, but I have to atone. I have to be happy with myself when I look in the mirror with clothes on or clothes off. I will lose weight when I need to or want to, but it will happen only when I choose. I refuse to listen to society tell me that I am not good enough.

This book is a seven-day self-esteem workbook and inspiration book for fat girls. It has day one through day seven listed along with seven inspirational boosts and actions that will help you begin to boost who you truly are in God's eye. This book has secrets on learning to manage your weight as well as learning to shape your body. It focuses on finding the beauty within us as well as helping us decide to get up and live in our heavy shoes because no one can do that the way we can as fat girls.

Confidence

When we hear the word confidence, we immediately think of boldness and of one being comfortable in one's skin: the way one looks, talks, and the way one carries oneself while walking. And when we think of a confident girl or woman, the fat girl never comes to mind. People hardly associate being big or fat with confidence. When a fat girl is being described, we hear words like ugly and sloppy, but rarely beautiful or confident. What is confidence and how do we know that we have it? Is a confident person the slender, petite or muscular person?

For too long, society has conditioned our thinking in the direction that for you to be confident, you need to be slim and muscular. You need to have a flat tummy, a defined waistline, not so big butt, and pointed, not too big breasts. But is this really what confidence is all about, physical appearance? I doubt it. Listen, we are all beautiful in our own ways, but confidence is not all about physical appearance. Yes, your physical appearance has a part to play in your degree of confidence—which is why I am writing this book to you—but confidence is so much more than just physical beauty, and it is very important to me that you become aware of this reality.

By definition, confidence is the ability to believe in yourself and your self-worth. It is the acknowledgment and awareness of your intrinsic worth as a human being, so that even when other people try to make you believe that you are worthless, you merely shrug it off because you are already aware that you are fundamentally good-to-go! You have to believe in and assure yourself that you are enough whether big, fat, or small. Never buy the lie that you are not good enough because you are bigger than society's idea of the perfect body size. Confidence is having a healthy self-esteem and self-image. You must believe in yourself and in your ability to be a confident person.

You need that to be able to do anything worthwhile in life.

For instance, your self-esteem must be high for you to participate in sporting activities or attend a tryout. Would a person who did not believe that they had what it takes attend tryouts? Would an applicant apply for a job if they felt they were not capable of performing the job? So you have to, first of all, believe in yourself, fat or not. You have to believe in the fact that your physical appearance has little or nothing to do with your self-worth and should not determine your level of confidence. And, for crying out loud, we are talking about just body size here. If you as a fat girl shrink yourself because of how you look, what would you expect handicapped people to do? But history has witnessed that even people with no arms and legs have stepped ahead of their handicap and achieved firsts that have left the world in awe. So, what do we say about you who have all your body parts intact and your only problem is that you have a generous share of body size?

Confidence is turned on automatically when you believe that you have what it takes to live your life. It could be something as simple as wearing a beautiful dress, high heels, or even a bathing suit. It takes confidence to step out in certain clothes, especially if you are a larger woman. If you are like me, wearing bathing suits may not come easily for you. I have thunder thighs and have always felt insecure about them. There are other fat women, on the other hand, who will boldly wear their bathing suits and strut along. That's what I am talking about: the ability to put on a bathing suit if I want to or have a need to regardless of my body size. That is confidence. It is confidence because I am no longer thinking about people's opinion about my appearance. I am doing it for me and not for anyone else.

Confidence is doing our thing without worrying about what people may think or say. When we begin to build confidence, we have to simply be ourselves and move regardless of the odds. We have to move regardless of gossip. We have to move regardless of our stretch marks, cellulite, dimples, and dents. Beauty is within the eyes of the beholder, and you are the most important beholder of your beauty. Confidence is loving yourself, flaws and all. Women, it is time to relax more when we talk about our flaws and celebrate them. As a fat girl, I have experienced negative comments and feedback from others. I am a woman who has grown tired of false illusions of what we as women should look like. I have had disagreements with men and women about my body type. I am proud of who God created me to be. I am not stressing myself out anymore trying to be what the world expects me to be. I am great just the way I am, and if I want to make changes to my body, the decision will be all mine. I am writing this book to help you heal and change your mindset about your weight and to help you build self-esteem. Confidence is a skill or ability that we all have, but it is up to you to use it.

A Fat Girl's Confidence

From the introduction and the title of this book, I am sure you are now well aware that the person writing to you is a fat person, a fat girl; I have battled with my weight for the greater part of my life. But what you may not know is my fat girl's secrets that have kept me from having low self-esteem or hating myself. I look at myself as a beautiful woman just like anyone else skinny or big. I wrote this book for all the fat girls in the world who have ever felt ugly. It is filled with inspirational self-study material. I want to let you in on how I did it so that you too can become comfortable and confident in your skin. I will be taking you on a seven-day journey of self-discovery, self-acceptance, and self-appreciation. We shall work on both your inner beauty and your outward appearance with the declarations and activities packaged for the next seven days.

Throughout this week, I want you to think about these words: fat and confident, fat and happy, and God made this fat. These words speak power to your life. Not only are you acknowledging your size, but you are adding value to it by accepting what God has made. Starting today, we are going to have fun with being who we are and not listening to other people's judgment of us.

Day One
I Love Me

Affirmation: *Look into the mirror today and say seven times to yourself, "I love me".*

I will ask you a question, and I want you to answer it sincerely: Do you love yourself? When you look in the mirror, do you appreciate what you see? I am not talking about you posting all over social media with the hashtags self-love and self-crush meanwhile, you cannot stand the sight of anything about yourself. No. What I mean is, do you truly love yourself, faults and all? If you do not, you will inadvertently give off the same energy of self-hatred to people around you, who will, in turn, see you the way you see yourself. Yes, people take you as seriously as you take yourself.

Now it is okay if, up to the point of your

encounter with this book, you have not come around to liking yourself because, sincerely, you do not love what you see in the mirror. I have stepped in to show you how to develop that self-love and self-acceptance.

Am I Fat or Overweight?

There is a big difference between being fat and being overweight. Fat is just one of the varieties of body types, just like we have fair or dark for skin color types. There is absolutely nothing wrong with being a fat person. In fact, when a naturally fat person loses weight up to the point of becoming thin, there is a problem. I know it is difficult to absorb this information because society has filled us with the belief that if you do not look like that thin girl on the cover of the magazine, there is something wrong with you. God, the Creator, loves variety and has made us in different shapes and sizes, but society is insisting that we should all be the same size. Make a decision not to listen to society.

Overweight, on the other hand, is a medical condition where you have outgrown the size your body can carry. It is a disorder. When overweight gets out of control, it becomes obesity. And my dear, trust me, you do not want to be obese.

I have made these distinctions so that we will be clear about the issue of self-love. If you are overweight, there is absolutely nothing to love about it; no this is not a case of you are beautiful just the way you are. Let us not be in denial here, please. If you are overweight, you should work on yourself and get back to that level of fatness that your body can carry, the way God made you. And when you have done that, you can boldly look in the mirror and love what you are seeing. And if you are just fat and not overweight, you have the right to love your weight no matter what anyone else thinks about it.

As a fat girl, if you still have difficulty loving your physical appearance, you need to work on your self-esteem. And while you are at it, make sure to take your self-care very seriously. Take your bath regularly (at least twice a day), always use deodorant, body spray, and perfume. Apply cosmetic products that will make you look even better; you know, when you look better, you feel better. Look in the mirror now and tell yourself that you love you. Take care of your hair. Style it differently today: add a bow, ribbon, hair band or something. If you are not hair savvy, make a hair appointment for the seven days of this confidence boost.

Activity Day 1:

- Getting up is a big part of your day. Most times when the alarm goes off, we wish we never have to do another twenty-four hours of hustling and bustling; but we have to do it anyway. Today is the first of the seven-day activities you shall be doing, so I encourage you to get off that bed right away!

- You are fully awake now, and the next thing on the list is to check your weight. Check it and write down what you weigh today. You are writing it down because this is the day you decide that your weight is enough! From now on, you will wear your weight boldly, in all confidence, regardless of what the next person thinks.

- Now that you have accepted your weight, you are going to take some necessary measures to maintain your confidence. And there is no better way of gaining and maintaining confidence than doing the right thing. To remain physically beautiful, you have to keep fit. Keeping fit is not just for physical appearance, it improves and maintains your overall well-being. So today—and from now on—you will do at least thirty minutes of exercise. Please do not get scared at the mention of the word exercise. It does not have to be rigorous. You can jog or take walks. Better still, there are exercise guides everywhere on the internet that you can download and follow religiously. Another option is for you to dance. Turn on your favorite music and dance until you are all sweaty. Whichever one you decide to go for, just make sure you exercise.

- Proceed to the bathroom to take a bath or a shower, after which moisturize your skin with some lotion. Put perfumed lotion on the outside of the thighs and under your curves and rolls. I know it's a job when you have all that body to moisturize. I am one who gets tired after my long shower, so I usually forget my lotion and perfume self-care moments. Silly me. If you get tired after having a bath or a shower as well, you are not alone. I prefer a bath to a shower any day. Once I step out of the bath, I feel brand new. Begin to style your hair after the bath or shower. Put on clean and matching underwear. No matter how clean you look on the outside, if your underwear is dirty, you are dirty, and you will lose confidence. Put on the kind of underwear that if for some crazy reason everybody is asked to strip to their underwear in public, you can boldly take off your clothes and display your underwear (That is probably never going to happen, anyway). Make sure you are wearing the right size of underwear; wearing the wrong size can make you look shapeless. Put on the kind of clothes and shoes you are comfortable in. Pick clothes for your comfort and not for trend. The kind of shoes you wear also goes a long way in making or breaking your level of confidence. Do you want to wear flats or heels? Are your shoes too tight or too loose? Then put on some makeup today. If you are a no makeup girl, add accessories that make you bold. (Remember, big is bold so be proud.)

- Proceed to the kitchen to make yourself some breakfast. Think of healthy choices with food for the week. Do not eat too much, neither should you eat too little. Have some moderate quantity of food.

- Generally, watch what you eat throughout

the day. Do not indulge in unnecessary snacking. If you want to snack, please go for fruits and nuts, and avoid pastries, chocolates, bread, and other snacks that have the propensity to fatten you. Avoid skipping meals; skipping meals can make you hunger for unhealthy snacks. Eat three times today, and, most importantly, drink plenty of water. It helps you stay hydrated and get a boost of energy. Today, if you have the option of using the elevator or climbing up stairs, please ignore the elevator and go with the stairs. Have fun today. Laugh, play, listen and learn something new. Learn that the word fat is just a word. It is an innocent word that describes your beautiful body type, though society has infused it with negative connotations. Ignore society. You will have to learn to ignore negative vibes if you are serious about being a confident, fat girl. Fat girls being comfortable with being called fat is a major confidence trophy. Believe that the people viewing fat as negative are merely ignorant and need some education. Remember, those words can't hurt you if you don't let them.

Day Two
I Am Enough

Affirmation: *Look into the mirror today and repeat seven times, "I am enough".*

The next thing you need to do after genuinely beginning to love yourself is to come to the awareness that you are enough. The most important step towards developing the fat girl's confidence is for you to deliberately stop wallowing in self-pity. You do not need anybody's validation to be able to live, so please stop seeking it. Our problem as fat girls lies in the fact that we do not believe that we are enough; we seek validation from just about anyone around us, both from people we know and people we do not know: parents, siblings, husbands, boyfriends, friends, foes, social media friends, social media strangers, and the list goes on!

You are an entity, a full-blown woman with a developed mind. You have all it takes to make choices and decisions about your life and take responsibility accordingly. The sooner you begin to learn how to use that basic human right, the better for you and all of us. The person you are seeking validation from is human just like you. They probably are merely just more confident than you, which is why you need to start working on your self-confidence immediately. Treat it as a matter of urgency.

Take, for instance, if you as a fat girl make healthy choices with your meals and exercise regularly, you will be fat but fit. Meanwhile, a slim girl who makes all the poor choices with her meals and never exercises because she believes that exercise is meant for fat people who are trying to lose weight, will be unfit; thin, unfit and unhealthy. But you will be busy admiring her life and wishing you were her just because of what you see on the outside. You will wish you were somebody you are healthier than. Meanwhile, in the grand scheme of things, good health is always placed above physical appearance. So, do well to concentrate on yourself. By yourself, I do not mean your physical appearance alone. Be cognizant of every part of your being as an organic whole.

Remember, God made you in His image, and that is all that matters. Nobody else's opinion about the way they think you should look matters. If you like what you see when you look in the mirror, that is good enough. Today, look into the mirror and say, "I am enough". Say it seven times and repeat the action as often as you can throughout the day. Don't forget to exercise, practice your new self-care routine, eat, pray, and slay.

Activity Day 2:

- Today you will pull out all your underwear; its underwear check day! You see, this is very important in any fat girl's life. I know that many of you have mix-matched underwear. I do, too. How many of you have to deal with sagging breasts syndrome? I do. Yes, big breasts are a heavy weight that is a hassle to secure in a bra. Take out your best bra, the one where your breasts sit up. Take out your control underwear that secures your stomach and helps push it in. Discard all old and loose underwear and get ready to shop for new ones.

- If you have panty girdles, corsets, and waist trainers, these work well too. If you don't have them, do not worry, I have recommendations for you and it is not too expensive. Walmart sells the best cupid panty girdles along with the 24 hr support plugged bras. Make sure to pick the one that will give your breasts the cone shape. Visit my website www.patriceshavone.com for corsets and fancy lingerie. I also use Adore Me; they have good panties for fat girls along with matching bras. You may be asked to sign up for membership at Adore Me. They have waist shapers that can be customized, and they also provide you with insight on waist training. My website www.patriceshavone.com has cheaper trainers with very supportive panty girdles. They begin the process of giving your body the perfect shape. If you get hemorrhoids, it means you picked the wrong type or the wrong size. If it is too tight, please take it off. Feel free to reach out to me on my social media handles if you need some help with picking the right underwear for you. Also, beware of latex allergies. I have my shapers hitting the market very soon. I have more insights that can help you, no matter your body type. Now, shaping your body is a major confidence trophy that will definitely bring a smile to your face. Shapers have to be used repeatedly. If you cannot wear a shaper for eight hours, try it for at least two hours a day.

Day Three
I Am Happy With Me

Affirmation: *Repeat seven times today, "I am sick and tired of trying to get other people to like me. It is time I show them that I am not going to change how I am unless I want to or there is a need to. No degree of fat shaming will ever make me change myself. I will not let them talk me down with their hurtful words. I will shrug it off, raise my shoulders high, and walk like the princess that I am. For as long as I do not take notice of them, their words have no hold on me. They can only succeed in making me miserable if they get me to believe that because I am fat, I should be unhappy. But I know that this is not true. I am fat, I am beautiful; I am happy with me!"*

Today's declaration is pretty lengthy, and you may need to look into the book as you speak confidence into your life. Take these declarations seriously because they are a vital part of your walk into a fat girl's confidence.

Activity Day 3:

- Gather your perfumes, body spray, deodorant, bath salts or green alcohol. Do you have a perfume collection? For instance, something like Elizabeth Taylor White Diamonds. Many people ask me what fragrance I wear. You know, I love White Diamonds because I am a diamond in the rough! I also love Versace fragrances; they are great, though expensive. Now is your time to shine just like you always imagined.

- Today, you will bathe and moisturize your skin, then put on your favorite fragrance. You may even experiment with fragrances. It is okay if you want to use two. I mix mine as well. Throughout the day you should smell and feel good. So, if you smell good, make sure you feel good. If you smell good and feel good, then you have to look good.

- Buy yourself fresh flowers and smell them. Close your eyes and imagine a beautiful you. Imagine being happy with being fat, imagine seeing others accept you for being you (fat). Fat, that's how you are. Get used to hearing the word fat; it no longer hurts you. The more familiar and relevant the word fat is in your mind and heart the less it will hurt you. Think of it as someone picking on you calling you fat but you do not hear them or feel hurt because you are comfortable with the words fat and how you are. This week you will build your self-esteem because strength must begin with you. The fact of the matter is you must learn to accept all bad things that could be thrown at you. All negative jokes about fat people must be okay with you, and it must begin today.

Day Four
I Am Fat And (not but) Happy

Affirmation: *Repeat seven times today as you look into the mirror, "I am built for this life; if not, God would not have blessed me".*

In the previous chapter, we agreed that coming to terms with the fact that the word fat is just a mere description of a body type. This is a big step towards developing the fat girl's confidence. Most fat girls have not made peace with that word, and for as long as they allow themselves to be haunted by the word, they will keep having problems with being fat and will never be confident. Nobody is comfortable using the word fat. Nowadays people, out of fake politeness, dread mentioning the word directly, they would rather resort to using euphemisms like a big girl and a plus-size girl. The word fat is dreaded. Why is this? This is why fat girls who have made peace with their body size tend to announce that they are fat but happy. Why the but?

If we are going to declare that we are happy with our body size, dear fat girls, why declare it as fat but happy? Why not fat and happy? The word "but" is a negative conjunction which shows that the expression preceding it does not agree with the one that follows it. But that is not true in our case. Fat and happy are not mutually exclusive terms.

Come to think of it, very sincerely now, when people call you fat, lazy, and sloppy, do they call you that because they are looking for things to say, or are you lazy and sloppy? I want you to shut this book right now, pause for a while and ponder on this question. It is not enough to want people to like you and be nice to you when you are neither likable nor nice to yourself. It is not acceptable. I am a fat girl like you. I know that our body weight has the tendency to make us sluggish, but if you form a habit of getting up and doing things, your brain registers that and your body responds accordingly.

Do not be a couch potato and expect people to follow you, singing your praises. No. It does not work that way, and I am not here to pamper you. You can't be pampered into confidence; you work your way into it. The point is, people, treat you the way you teach them to, and you teach them by merely playing the part. If they see you being lazy and sloppy, they will treat you like a lazy and sloppy person; but if they see you always on your feet taking care of yourself and things, they will show you the respect you deserve. It is also true that some people may still see negativity in your positive attitude, but when you are sure you are doing the right thing, forget them. It is not your fault that they are always wired to be negative, and their words can have little or no effect on you.

So, now that you have accepted that being fat is no longer a curse in your life and you are learning to accept your reality of being fat and being confident anyway, you can go ahead and set up some weight loss goals, if you think you need to shed some pounds. On the other hand, if losing weight is not what you want, then maintain your current body size and make sure you do not become overweight. It is safe to say you are confident in your fat skin. Get up and get ready, beautiful fat girl!

Activity Day 4:

- On this fourth day, you will gather all your nice shoes together: heels and flats. As a fat girl, I know your feet hurt from time to time. One of your issues may be not putting on heels at all because of your weight. I was a fat girl afraid to wear heels, and after buying the Dr. Scholl's products, my feet were still hurting. Upon research, I ordered Torrid shoes. Torrid is better, but be sure that the height of the shoes are made in such a way that you can walk in them. I suggest nothing over 2½ inch heels. Clarks is a game changer for all fat girls in the world. Clarks has pumps that are comfortable. Guess what this fat girl did in her Clarks? Danced and stood up in them for hours and had an amazing time! Secrets of fat girl shoes are to be level and balanced. Wedges should be one of your best friends as well. Wedges help you maintain your comfort throughout the day even as you look pretty.

- Make sure you pair your shoes with a matching outfit. You should set aside one pair of casual flats, then nice yet comfortable heels. Make sure you set aside a nice dress and walking shoes. At the beginning of the day, you will do 30 minutes of walking. Now, as you walk imagine yourself like a queen. Fat girls can dress and be cute; do not let anyone else tell you otherwise. Throughout the day, please remind yourself of being fat AND happy. When your feet start hurting, say I am fat, and yes my feet hurt but I feel happy today. You will get used to it in a little time. Heels are usually uncomfortable to anybody when worn for the first time, irrespective of their body size. So it is not solely a fat girl's predicament.

- Most importantly, you were born to be seen because big is bold. People see us, even when they do not want to because we are big, and we are beautiful!

Day Five
I Am Somebody; I Matter, I Am Free

Affirmation: *Repeat 7 seven times today as you look into the mirror, "I am carefully, wonderfully, and beautifully made. I am important. I will let no one look down on me".*

As fat girls in a society that has little tolerance for fat people, we wear the shoes, and we know where they hurt. Even when we begin to accept our body size, there are still pointers all around us, reminding us that our body is not acceptable by society. But it should not be so. We should not let society look down on us because we are not what it wants us to be. There is no one standard for beauty. There is no perfect body size. Why should we pick a particular body size and want all other varieties to conform to this one size? Does it even make sense? Everybody cannot be slim; do not let slim people bully you into thinking that something is wrong with you just because you are fat. Do you know that the models you see on TV screens and on the covers of magazines are performing? Do you want to compare your natural look with their performance? And let me tell you again, do not think that being fat is a huge problem just because people make fun of you. It is not your fatness that is prompting them to talk about you; it is that primordial inability of human beings to mind their business because even if you were thin, they would still make fun of you for being thin. So you see, the problem is not your body but their mouths. And there is no way you can help them. Just try to find a way to hear them talk and be happy anyway.

As you are going through the process of floating above all the negativities that society may throw at you, it is also important to not be in a box all by yourself. Try to associate with other fat girls who are going through similar challenges, so that you can share your experiences, learn from them, encourage, and be there for one another.

Be happy in the clothes you choose to wear. Do not choose any item of clothing just because it is trending. That is a no-no! Pick clothes that agree with and flatter your unique body type. Wear your fatness so well that anybody who looks at you would almost wish they had the same body type as you, so they could fit into that dress you are rocking. That is the goal, girl! Stop trying to look like the next girl (who probably wishes she looked like you, anyway!). Clothes are a huge obstacle in a fat girl's life. I remember when it was very hard to find clothing sizes for fat girls. How are fat models labeled? At a shopping size of four and above, you see there are still issues in the fat girls' department. So, it is okay to make clothes for fat girls but not hire the actual fat girl models that buy sizes 16 plus. But thank God the world of fat girls now has a new definition; we can walk into clothing stores and pick up clothing items of our sizes.

Clothing was always an issue for me growing up. I could never find cute clothes for my body. I do remember going into Lane Bryant's but did not like the sizes of their clothes. To me, they had no shape. So here are some secret places to shop. I shop at Dot's, Cato's and Ashley Stewart's. Patrice Shavone is an excellent place to shop as well, along with other online boutiques for fat girls, like Curvaceous Boutique, which has great sales. But try to order maybe a size up for a better fit. Shun Melson is another great site you will spend your money on and get value for, but order a size down with this boutique. Ashley Stewart is a nice fat girl clothing store but be sure not to pick up too many items because prices there can be tricky. It is very easy to spend two hundred dollars at this store within an hour by accident. You are now aware of six secret stores where fat girls buy beautiful clothing. You will be transformed into a beautiful princess or queen with these online sites. Consider yourself blessed with this information all fat girls should be aware of all. Do not forget to go to www.patriceshavone.com and make your online purchases to support my clothing line

Never restrict your look, voice, laughter, dance or beauty to please others. God has crafted you perfectly, and no one on this earth was created with the same features as you (unless you have an identical twin).

Activity Day 5:

- Today is outfit day! Pick up two outfits: one, a nice dress; and the second, jeans with a nice casual shirt. Remember, we are bold and beautiful fat girls. Boldness springs from our amazing ability to style our big bodies and step into places with our heads held high.

- Walk out of the house today a brand-new woman full of confidence and ready to take on the world. You should start with the casual outfit for your workplace or school. After which you will step into your fabulous dress. You should consider this a date with yourself. Go to dinner, a movie, or a comedy show. Now for my younger ladies, tonight you will attend a night out with friends, maybe a dance. The purpose of tonight is to get up and go out of the house. This activity is to inspire you always to feel free to step out with confidence in public.

Day Six
I Am Loved

Affirmation: *Repeat seven times today as you look into the mirror, "I am smart, I am bold I am beautiful, I am brave, I am loved, I have peace".*

Have you ever lost a relationship because of your body size? Has someone ever walked out of your life because you are fat? You are not alone my dear; it happens to fat girls all over the world. It has been said that it is not what happens to you in life but how you react to it that matters. That someone rejected you does not mean you should also reject yourself.

One of the downsides of being a fat girl is that when men look at you, they are most likely going to lust after your body before even having the chance to encounter your personality. It is said that men are moved by what they see; if we are to go by this assertion, then fat girls have more battles than thin girls in that respect. The female body has been made very soft and attractive to every normal man; and as fat girls tend to have bigger breasts and butts, they are naturally forced to put extra effort in directing the attention of men away from their body and onto themselves and the values they have to offer.

Back to the question of rejection from men; it is well known that just as society has projected slim girls as the standard for beauty, most men prefer slim girls. Slim is seen as sexy while fat is sloppy. But then we see that some men go after the fat girl, and when this girl accepts him, after a while, he expects her to shrink herself into a slimmer figure. But why is this so? You saw her as fat as she was and you went ahead to ask her out, now you are asking her to change herself because of you? How is that fair? Listen, ladies, do not struggle to get slim when you are naturally a fat person all because of a man. He saw you the way you were before he came to you, and if he suddenly cannot deal with your size anymore, it means he is not consistent, and you should not be with that kind of person, anyway. If you succumb to his wishes, he will find something else in the near future that he will want you to change about yourself. A man like that cannot stand by your side if you are experiencing postpartum depression after childbirth. Let him go. Very soon, love shall find you; and when it does, your body size shall not be a barrier. Do not shrink yourself because of a man. Do not let a man give you conditions. Do not let a man treat you less than you deserve. Let him go. It may not be easy, but the earlier you let what was never meant to be in your life go, the better prepared you will be to receive your own man when he comes.

As you think about this sixth day, remember to make the affirmations as you pray and before you go to bed. As a confident, big, and beautiful young woman, it is important to feed yourself with words of love and confidence to keep the big girls' attitude going. You see, this is a movement for fat girls who were never given a chance on TV screens and magazines; a movement for girls who the men in their lives were ashamed to claim as their girlfriends, wives, or just plain friends.

I want you to think of yourself as one among other big girls, BBW's, and a real woman with rolls and curves who acknowledge themselves as God's masterpiece and go ahead to fulfill the purpose for which they have been created regardless of their body size or what people make of it. No longer shall we feel ashamed for being a size bigger than the average beauty queens. Remember you are capable of being married, having a great relationship, landing that big job, or being on TV and in magazines if that is what you want. If they tell you otherwise, just remind them about some of those fat people that are in their own family. You see, being fat is not a new thing, it is just being looked at as a bad thing by unthinking people. It's okay to be happy and fat and love yourself.

Now I know that some people out there may think that the fat girl's declaration of self-acceptance is done in denial. But that is not true. It took us so long to come to this point where we are saying that we are beautiful just the way we are. Some may say it is not true because being fat makes one susceptible to health issues like diabetes. But it is true because there are many thin diabetic patients out there; both fat and thin people need to take care of themselves to avoid health challenges. Being thin does not exempt you from health challenges.

We need to stop acting as though it is a crime for someone to be bigger than what society accepts as the standard, and stop thinking that everyone has to be a certain size to be beautiful in our eyes. Stop letting others feel badly for the way they are because they were made in God's image like you—another variety of God's image. It does not pay to hurt other people through our words and actions and make them feel badly for the way they were created. It does not make sense.

So, dear fat girl, be happy with who you are, love the big girl you are and stand tall as no one can love you the way you do.

Activity Day 6:

- Today you will spend two hours putting together all the steps that you have learned from day 1 through day 5. This includes hair, makeup, shoes, and outfits, not forgetting your shapewear. You will begin today as a day for relaxing at home. Grab candles, bubble bath, play some soothing music, or read a nice book. You will spend the next thirty minutes in the tub meditating on who you currently are and imagining yourself in the future you want, exactly the way you want it to be.

- Dream of yourself as a beautiful woman who is leading others with boldness into the peaceful realm of self-discovery and self-mastery. In doing this activity myself, I became bold as I started creating my path to unlock the true me.

- Next, you will get your day started by completing the following steps you have been following from day 1 through day five. Observe your new self-care ritual again: bath/shower, moisturizer, clean and fitting underwear, makeup if needed, hair care, a casual dress, and of course shoes. Never forget to use your deodorant, body spray, and perfume. You can go ahead now and step out in style; you are beautiful!

- Today you will leave your home feeling confident and ready to engage in activities that are different from what your regular day looks like. Visit the art gallery, try visiting the lake, go for a walk in the park and meditate throughout the day. Chant the words "I am loved, I am smart, I am bold, I am beautiful, I am brave, I have peace, I am great". Spend 30 minutes alone in peace and think about who you truly are. See yourself the way God sees you, not the way society does. No matter how big you may be, you are God's little princess.

- You are no longer battling with depression or identity crisis. You love yourself and you are loved by those who truly matter in your life. As you make this affirmation to yourself, believe it with all your heart and mind and soul. Spend the rest of the day around friends or family who show you the love you need and deserve. Place your focus on the people who believe in you and breathe life into your body and mind. These are the people who want you to beat depression, low self-esteem, and identity issues. You have been able to achieve that, and you should let them see the happy side of you.

You see if we continue to listen to this world that is full of confusion, the same world that tells us we should not eat this but continue to sell it in the market; the world with ever-changing standards, we all would feel badly about our lives and self. Today, that old person is dead; no longer will she live within you. You are now brave and capable of anything as you should have always been. Let that fat girl beauty shine through for the world to see. I know how I used to feel until I made up my mind to embrace the true me. And as the queen that I have realized I am, I can no longer let empty people determine what they think is the best for me. Yes, I said it; they are empty. Fat girls stay full and fluffy. Who wants to live an empty life? Definitely not this fat girl! I say that confidently because I am me and please believe I am a one of a kind type of beauty queen!

Day Seven Affirming your Confidence

Affirmation: *Repeat seven times today as you look into the mirror, "I am confident, I am beautiful, I am happy with me, and I believe in myself".*

Today is the day that you shall gain victory! Shout victory three times; the old you is gone. You are now confident; you can now wake up each day and beautify yourself. You now realize that you are completely in love with who God has created you to be. You should now accept who you are as a person and let no one belittle you. If they do, find three jokes to get back at them. Remember, everyone has flaws; find theirs and go for it. Laugh for the rest of your days here on earth. You matter you are needed, you are special, and you are like no one else in this world; a prized gem carefully crafted by the hands of God. You possess great qualities outside of the physical appearance. Let people shake in their shallowness as you move on with accepting yourself for who you are (bold and beautiful) because you were born that way. Shake that fat every chance you get. Go out and dance, sing, laugh and make friends. Talk when you want to, and let no one shut you up. Do not let people take your joy away from you.

Day 7: Activity

- Today you need to relax, attend church, make a speaking engagement, read something inspirational, sing inspirational songs and keep the inspiration within your heart and mind at all times. By the end of the day, find a sexy, revealing outfit; put it on and relax. Stare at your sexiness in the mirror.

- Remember the purpose of this book is to motivate you into feeling better about yourself. Find a nice fat baby doll gown to lie in, even if you are lying alone. Get that nice glass of wine and relax tonight. I have a line of lingerie products that is magic for fat women. Visit www.patriceshavone.com for great deals; nothing is over twenty dollars. To build your self-esteem, repeat the steps you learned throughout this workbook, and watch out for other books and readings by me.

You Are More than How You Look

On a general note I want you, my now beautiful, confident, fat girl to know that paying too much attention to your body size can distract you from doing the things that matter in life. Your confidence should not be anchored on physical appearance alone. A perfect body with nothing on the inside is as good as useless and is a distraction to both you the carrier and to the people who will look at you.

You may be wondering why then did she spend a whole book talking to me about my physical appearance only to turn around to say it is much more than that? I did because I know where the problem is coming from. I have been there, and I know all about fat-shaming and what it is capable of doing to a lady who has not yet made peace with the fact of her fatness. I know about the several attempts to eat less and exercise more, the hunger to look like that girl on the cover of the magazine, the days of depression, and the hopelessness of it all. But all these are because society will not let us wear the body God has given us, and wear it in peace. That is why I have spent time giving you tips on how to get yourself out of the rot of hopelessness and into the light where you belong.

But then, should we really let society make us focus too much attention on our body? Should we let society make us take our minds away from things that matter in life? Your answer is as good as mine.

Now that you have made peace with your body, I want you to take your eyes away from that body and focus it on something else. This does not mean that you should stop following your self-care routine or ignore your health. Still, do your routine; do it until it becomes a habit. And at each point, know that you are doing this for yourself and not because of anyone else. By the time your new routine has become a habit, you will need to take your mind off your body; keep taking care of yourself, but do not think about it too much. What should you be thinking about?

I want you to think about ways to improve your life. Ask yourself, in what ways can I add value to my life and the world at large? What are those things you can do now that people will remember you for when you are no longer here? The first step towards getting the answer to this question is for you to deliberately put efforts into improving yourself. What do you do with your life on a daily basis? What does your regular day look like? Besides your job (if you have one), what else? Do you go out of your way to improve your life? If you sit in front of the TV every day watching movies and soaps, that is not a good use of your time. Movies are good (some of them, anyway), but we all know that too much of anything is bad.

There are different aspects that come together to make up your life as an organic whole, and if you neglect any of the parts, the other parts of the whole will suffer. I am talking about the mental, spiritual, social, financial, and of course physical aspects. For the mental, what do you feed your mind with? It is what goes into your mind that will come out through your mouth as words, and the kind of words you use reflects the quality of person you are. You need to be conscious of what goes into your mind. Too many movies are not good for your mental health. There are healthier alternatives like books. When was the last time you picked up a book to read? You can learn a lot by reading good books. You can travel around the world through books, and you can meet many wise people who are no longer alive but have their words still breathing within books. A saying goes that true intelligence is not in knowing everything about a little thing, rather, it knows a little about everything. Your ability to be diverse in knowledge is a plus for you. Reading books helps you to become a more interesting person to be around because you will always be able to keep a conversation going through your wealth of diverse knowledge.

What about your spiritual life? As humans, we have a spiritual side to our being, and it cannot be neglected. Do you make time to commune with and worship the God who created you to be so beautiful and decorated you with so much intelligence, talents, and abilities? Or are you so busy that you do not have the time to notice Him? You should be grateful to God every day of your life for at least keeping you alive because it is only when you are alive that you can worry about all the things we have talked about in this book. And you should express your gratitude by making time to spend in the presence of your God.

One of the major characteristics that differentiate us from other animals is our need for community. What is your social life like? Do you have friends? How is your relationship with other members of your family? Are you a good person who genuinely cares about other people or is "me, myself and I" your favorite phrase? Nobody is an island. Nobody exists in a vacuum, and we are all products of our society. So, your relationship with people around you is a very important part of your existence that should not be neglected. Be deliberate about making yourself an interesting person to be around, and people around you are most likely going to return the favor.

All the suggestions outlined in this book can only be achieved with the help of money. You cannot buy your moisturizers, deodorant, body spray, hair cream and so on if you are broke. So the role of money cannot be overemphasized in a fat girl's life; and by money, I mean financial independence. You need to have some money of your own. You need to have a steady source of income. Some girls feel very free to depend on their parents or the men in their lives for money. It is okay when kids are financially dependent, but as a young woman, you cannot afford to not have your own money. In fact, having your own money is a very big confidence booster; you can buy whatever you want, whenever you want to buy it without anybody asking you questions. The reason some fat girls remain in relationships where they are forced to shrink themselves is that they cannot afford to leave, and I mean that literally. Get a job, make your own money, save, invest, and prepare yourself for the future.

And finally, it is also not all about you. It has been confirmed over and over again that the more you invest in other people, the happier you become. There is a certain kind of joy that comes to your heart when you have put a smile on someone else's face, and the major way to leave your foot prints in the sands of time is by touching as many lives as possible. That is one way to immortalize your name. So, as you are investing in yourself, also reach out to other people. Look out for the poor around you, the orphans, motherless babies, widows, and the less privileged in general. We change the world by changing our immediate environment. If everybody changes their immediate environment, then we have changed the world.

An open letter to confident Ladies

Dear confident and happy fat girl, it is important for me to let you know that your life is more than what you see. There are many other aspects to your life that are all a part of the outcome of what is visible to you. Because you can see just your body, that is the part you easily want to take care of. But you also have a mind, a soul, and a spirit, which all combine to make up your complete being, and if you neglect any part of them, the other parts will inadvertently be affected. When your mind is in distress, your body feels it; when your spirit is troubled, your entire being is troubled.

So, this is why you have to pay as much attention to all areas of your being as you pay to your body which you see. We shall go ahead now and discuss ways in which you can achieve this.

Your Thoughts; Pen Them Down

As you go about your day to day activities, you will have different thoughts clamoring for your attention; Some of them are positive, while many others are negative. It is always advisable that you pen down these thoughts as much as you can, and I will tell you why:

4 Reasons You Need to Put Your Thoughts in Writing

- The major reason you need to write down your thoughts is that writing them down is a way of concretizing them for easy reference in the future. When you have written down your thoughts, you can go back to them later to compare with your new thoughts and evaluate and note whether you have been making progress or not in your thought processes. It is a good way to monitor your thought processes.

- Writing down your thoughts helps you to see in black and white the degree of how positive or negative your overall thinking processes are. If they are mostly positive, you will know that you are on the right track. But if they are mostly negative, then you will need to do something fast to make a change, because it is what goes on inside of you that eventually comes out for people to see.

- The daily writing of your thoughts is called journaling, and it has a positive psychological effect on your mental health and overall wellbeing. When you write down your thoughts, you are writing down your feelings, your pains, your joys, your cares, and your anxieties. And just like it is said that a problem shared is a problem half-solved, concretizing your thoughts gives it another form of existence and frees up your mind, at least a bit. And it helps reduce stress. There is a form of psychological release that you feel when you write down your thoughts; it feels almost as if you have just spoken to someone else. So, do well to pen down your thoughts and reap the benefits that come with that act.

- Again, it has been said that the shortest pencil is more reliable than the longest memory. Writing down your thoughts is one way to keep in touch with yourself and your mental development over time. If you write down your thoughts today and go back to them later in life, you will be amazed at how far you have come. And this will serve as some sort of encouragement for you to keep pushing.

More on Positive and Negative Thinking

As a fat girl who lives in a world that frowns at fatness, you may find yourself sometimes dwelling on the fact that you are fat; and if you have not already embraced that reality, your thoughts are most likely going to be negative. You will find yourself thinking; I am not good enough, I am ugly, I am lazy and sloppy, I never get anything done. And this is usually because these are the same things you have heard people say to you over and over again. But if you allow your thought process to remain like this, you are eventually going to destroy your own life. This is why you need that fat girl's confidence that will give you the courage to stay on the path of positive thinking.

When you write down your thoughts and notice

a regular pattern of negative thinking, you can stand up to those negative thoughts and tell them that they do not belong in your mind; there is no room for them there. And then you can gradually start building a habit of positive thinking. Whenever the negative thought of "you are not good enough" comes, you give a firm response of "that's a big lie; I am good enough! I am happy, I am confident, and you have to deal with that!" This is the kind of mindset the seven days of affirmations you have carried out at the beginning of this book will help you achieve.

3 Ways to Capture Your Thoughts

Before I go on to list some ways in which you can capture your thoughts, let me quickly add that writing down your thoughts will curb the rate at which idle thoughts fly through your mind. So, some of the ways you can capture your thoughts are:

Get a Notepad and a Pen: To make it a

beautiful experience, you should consider getting a beautiful notepad and a type of pen you can comfortably write with. These will even entice you to always want to write.

Get a Tablet: You can put your thoughts down on a tablet if writing with pen and paper comes off as unfashionable to you. If you do not have a tablet, you can pick up one you can afford from your favorite brand of electronics and go ahead to capture your thoughts.

Your Cell Phone: Your cell phone comes in handy for putting down your thoughts because it is something you can always carry around with you in your pocket. For instance, if you are travelling or merely in a vehicle going somewhere, you can always pick up your cell phone, click on the notepad icon and put down your thoughts at any time. Many people do not utilize this notepad in their cell phones; some have never even noticed it on their phones. But if you form a habit of journaling, you will always find yourself looking for white space to write down something, and since we are almost always with our cell phones, it is surely the easiest and most readily available writing tool for putting down your thoughts.

I also want you to note that each of these options has its own advantages and disadvantages. There is a possibility that you will lose the soft copy of your writings if they are not properly backed-up. And in the same way, your notepad can be destroyed by water or fire if not properly protected. Trust me, you do not want to lose your years of journaling that could bring back beautiful memories for you in the future.

Releasing Your Inner Energy

We are always more than we are willing to give ourselves credit for. You are more than what you think you are. There is so much power and untapped energy inside of you that has remained dormant because you probably do not even know that you have them. You are more than your job; you are more than your role in the family. You are even more than you allow yourself to dream. And to live life to the fullest, you have to step into the inner part of your consciousness and release your inner energy.

Look around you and see some miracles that came about because of science and technology. There is no science or technology without the actions of human beings; humans who sat down, searched within themselves and came up with things that help improve human existence, and even some that may lead to its destruction. These humans, at the time, utilized their inner energy; they listened to their inner selves and were able to create things. You too have the power to create or destroy, depending on how you choose to use your inner energy. Every human being has some bustling amount of inner energy that they either are not aware of or are channeling in the wrong directions.

What Happens When You Release Your Inner Energy

- Releasing your inner energy helps you to realize that you are so much more than the eyes can see. It helps you take your eyes off yourself and place them on things that matter. You will begin to appreciate yourself as not only someone made in the image of God but also someone who has been endowed with the same creative abilities as

God.

- Releasing your inner energy will help you discover more about yourself. If your life has always revolved around one area or around some particular things such as your job or career, raising a family etc., you will begin to appreciate yourself as someone who can be and do so much more. You will realize that your life is not tied to the routine of things you are already used to, and this will prompt you to reach out for more.

- Releasing your inner energy attracts you to positive forces that will help you enrich your life. If your life revolves around mundane things, it will also attract mundane things and people. But when you begin to tap into your inner energy, it comes off on the outside of you and attracts equally honorable things.

- Releasing your inner energy helps you to feel in charge of your life. It helps you to see life beyond the ordinary, and when you have reached that point where you become aware that there is so much more, you will no longer worry or care much about little things that do not matter. You will not let them take your time because now you have greater things to channel your energy into. That is when you will begin to feel in charge of your life and the things around you.

5 Ways to Release Your Inner Energy

- The first step towards releasing your inner energy is sincerity. Be sincere with yourself on your current state in life: the things you are doing right, the things you are getting wrong, and what you are willing to change about them all. When you have done this, you will have created a fertile ground for your inner energy or inner strength to thrive.

- Clear your mind of the things you have

allowed to form a clutter around. You are already aware of the act of putting down your thoughts, and that will help you fish out your thought patterns. So, clear your mind of every form of negativity. Your inner energy needs space to emerge. As you are clearing your mind, also clear your physical space. You cannot, as a matter of fact, have a clear mind if your surroundings are cluttered. Put everything around you in its place. This will help you feel relaxed. And when there is a release from stress like this, your inner energy will feel free to emerge.

- Step aside for a while and stay away from all forms of distraction. At this time, even positive things can be sources of distraction. You need to spend some time alone in total calmness and serenity so that you can be open to hear the part of your being that has been long shut-out by the noise in your day to day activities.

- Pray to your God or whatever it is you believe in. Your inner energy is beyond the physical, and you need to get to that realm beyond the physical and mundane to be able to access it in its fullness and harness all it has to offer. Devote yourself to prayer and meditations and reconnect with your spiritual source.

- When you have created this space and made your inner self-ready to contain your inner energy, you can then begin to visualize all the positive possibilities you can ever imagine for yourself. Remember, we said that the inventions you see around are a result of people who had one time or another removed their mind from the mundane things and channeled it towards releasing their inner energy, which empowered them with creative ability. This is the stage you have entered now. As soon as you have prepared your mind, it is ready to receive the inspiration that will start up the creative process that is inherent in all humans. Make sure your mind is open and ready for inner energy to thrive.

You Take Orders from Yourself Alone

Sweetheart repeat this to yourself, I am all the permission I need. I am all the approval I need. I am all the validation I need. I do not need to look elsewhere for validation.

Because of your being fat in a society that is intolerant of bigger body sizes, one will not be surprised if you have difficulty believing in yourself or have low self-esteem. For instance, you may always find yourself asking other people around you, do you think I've lost some weight? Does this dress look good on me? Do you think I should take that job? Do you think I am going to make a good mother? Can I wear a swimsuit in public? Can I? ....and the list goes on. You are never sure. You always look up to someone else to stamp a seal of approval on your life before you do anything. That way of life does not depict a confident woman, and it has to stop. You need to be a complete woman, one who can make choices and decisions all by herself and take full responsibility for her actions. That is who a confident fat girl is. She does not spend her life taking orders on how to live her life from people who care to dish them out. I repeat, you are all the permission you need.

I am not suggesting, mind you, that you should never take advice from other reasonable people. No, that is not what this is about. We are social beings who co-exist with other people and, since nobody knows it all, we should get advice from other people from time to time. But my emphasis is on the fact that you should have a mind of your own. You should not do things just because other people are doing them. You should have a reason and purpose for every action you take. Never do things just because every other person is doing them; you are not every other person. If you believe in yourself and in the fact that you are enough, you will always look inwards for answers and confirmations.

Never be afraid of what people may say. Most of the people you are worried about probably are not even thinking about you, so go ahead and do your stuff. And even if they are thinking about you, you do not owe them anything. You are not under any obligation to sacrifice your joy for people who contribute little or nothing to your existence. Okay, how many of the people you are worried about pay your bills? Even if they do, it is still not reason enough for you to go through life trying to please everybody. That is a terrible way to live. Whether you do what you want to do or not, people will still find faults in your life. So why don't you just go ahead and do you; do that which is in line with your purpose. You must have heard that if you do not want people to talk about you, 'do nothing, say nothing, and be nothing'. And I am pretty sure that is not what you want in your life. There are a lot of things you can be in this life, and you cannot afford to settle for anything. Brace up, go out and be yourself unapologetically.

7 Reasons You Don't Need to Seek External Approval

- You need to be yourself because, as the saying goes, everyone else is taken, you can't be anyone else. You can only imitate. And who wants to go through life living as fake? Definitely not you.

- You do not need external approval because you are all the permission you need. Waiting for other people to endorse your life before you begin to live is ridiculous. What if they do not care? Does it mean you are never going to live?

- Being yourself unapologetically has a way of releasing your locked up inner energy. We talked about sincerity as one of the requirements for releasing your inner energy earlier on and being yourself is the most basic form of sincerity to self.

- Living without seeking validation from other people makes them see you as someone they can look up to. It shows that you are unwavering in your ways and can be trusted. People will see you as someone who is worthy of being listened to. It shows that you are capable of having your own unbiased opinions and can be trusted to bring something meaningful to the table during conversations. People will respect you.

- Generally, there is something approval addiction does to your self-confidence. In fact, you won't be confident in yourself at all if you are always seeking other people's approval. You will end up placing yourself at the mercy of their every whim and caprices. And when they do not approve of you, you will wallow in self-pity. But being in charge of your life without seeking permission or approval from anybody makes you a confident person. You can make decisions on your feet without having to consult anybody on your approval list.

- When you live a life free from approval addiction, you will live fearlessly; you will know your capabilities and limitations and be able to trust yourself. You can always look back on how some decisions you have taken by yourself turned out well, and you can easily trust in your ability to do more and be more.

- Living a life free of approval addiction removes unnecessary anxiety from your life. When the first thing you are thinking about is not how to please everybody around you, you can become less hard on yourself and put aside some perfectionist tendencies that may have been holding you back.

Journal Groups: Growing Your Confidence Exponentially

One fact you should never get out of your mind as a fat girl is that in this fat girl's journey of yours, you are not alone. Other fat girls of this world are in the same situation as you, for society generally—regardless of race or geographical location—is not comfortable with fatness. So, never feel that the situation is peculiar to you. That said, I encourage you to seek motivation from other fat and confident girls around you who have embraced the fact of their fatness and remained cheerful despite society. Look for fat girls around you, maybe in your family, your workplace, your church, or even a celebrity you admire. Reach out to them and draw strength from them. You can also get motivated by reading books like this one of shared testimonies by fat girls who have pulled themselves out of the rot of society's expectations and into the light where they belong. You can reach out to me through my social media handles, and I will also do my best to guide you on any area you may be confused about. All I am saying, in a nutshell, is that many people have been there, many are still there, and you should reach out to them to draw strength. This brings us to the point of joining and building journal groups.

One of the many ways through which humans express their emotions is by writing. Writing is therapeutic; there is a healing effect that comes with pouring out your heart on paper. So, you are encouraged to keep a journal for writing down your day to day activities. We have also established that it is paramount for humans to embrace the community of their fellow humans, and not just that of their fellow humans, but also that of those who share similar interests with them. That way, they can build one another up.

As a fat girl, you need to be in the community of other fat girls who share the same interest with you so that you all can encourage and be there for one another. One effective way of keeping such group active is through journaling; call it a group or collective journaling. When you are in a journal group, you will have a regular platform for self-expression. Journal groups are not restricted to sharing selected experiences from their lives with one another, they most times share the things they have in their journals as well. This way, other members of the group will be able to monitor the progress of each member.

Benefits of Joining a Journal Group

- **Building Community:** The primary aim of a journal group is that you will find yourself in a community of people like you. And what this implies is that you will feel at home among them, you won't be afraid of being judged, and you can freely pour out your heart as you have always wanted to. We agreed earlier that you need to take some time off for yourself; a time when you are alone in the company of yourself to be able to reach your inner energy. This is not a contradiction to that exercise; it is only a way of striking a balance. If you are always alone without joining the company of your fellow humans, there won't be a balance, and you may lose touch with reality. Humans are social beings and that fundamental need for society should be respected. So, go ahead and join, not just any group, but a community of people like yourself. And since this is all about the fat girl's confidence, you are encouraged to join a journal group of fat girls.

- **Mutual understanding:** One of the benefits you will enjoy now that you have joined a journal group is mutual understanding. You all in the group have something in common: you are girls, and you are fat; and since you exist in a world that is not welcoming of fat people, you all will have a kind of we against the world feeling and understanding. You will understand one another's pains, joys, moods, and attitudes. This is something anybody would long for.

- **Shared Experiences:** One of the things that brought you together in your journal group is to share your experiences and learn from one another's experiences. When you are granted insight into the experiences of other members of your group, you will realize that the fat girl's experience is not peculiar to you, that it happens to other fat girls in the world. And this has a relieving effect, and it will give you the strength and willingness to keep up the struggle.

- **Listening and Being Listened to:** Your journal group or community is made up of people who are willing to listen to you because they understand you. They are not impatient when you are sharing your experience because they can relate, they know exactly where you are coming from.

And as humans, we need people willing and ready to listen to us. No matter how strong you may be, time and time again, you will need to talk, and you will need to have someone listen to you. That privilege of being listened to is one of the benefits you will get from being a member of a journal group.

- **Igniting Creativity:** Remember, journaling is writing; writing down your down your day to day experiences. So, as you write, you may find out along the line that you are beginning to develop an interest in the art of writing, and you may decide to pursue that area as well. Nothing stops you from becoming a writer. Too. if you find out that you have a flair for writing. In other words, a person who consistently keeps a journal may likely end up becoming a writer. And that is good.

- **Growth:** Generally, joining a journal group will lead to your growth, both personally and socially. First of all, joining a community of people means that you will be in close contact and interaction with these people on a regular basis, and this will help improve your social life. If you are someone who does not feel comfortable meeting people, you will gradually begin to develop that confidence, and that is a good development in the social aspect of your life.

- **Networking:** Besides sharing experiences, listening to one another, and encouraging one another, a journal group is an opportunity for networking. You may meet people in your line of career or business in your journal group and strike up some communication and relationship that could lead to a serious business partnership in the future.

This is all a tip of the iceberg when it comes to the importance of joining a journal group as a way of building the fat girl's confidence.

Activities for Journal Groups

- Members of the group should be made to write down their thoughts and experiences daily as a compulsory commitment as a member of the group. These writings are to be shared on the group's meeting days. The group is, after all, a journal group, and journaling is basically about writing.

- *Writing Assignments:* The group can assign weekly or monthly tasks for every member to monitor their overall wellbeing. It may be accounts of the highlights of their week or a summary of how the week went.

- *Individual Presentations:* The group can assign topics to every member of the group to develop and present during their meeting days. It could be topics related to their struggle or about other things entirely for diversification. Little awards could be given to the members who give the best presentations. This activity will be a major confidence booster to members of the journaling group because it is training on public speaking. Anyone who can speak boldly in public is a confident person.

- *Visitation:* The group should take turns in paying visits to all members of the group as a way of building a bond and making a family out of the journal group. People like being thought about or remembered. Members who are sick or do not make it to the meeting for one reason or the other should be paid a visit.

- *Games:* The group members can play games during some of their meeting days as a way of adding fun to the group activities. This can be a part that will make people look forward to the group meeting days.

- *Community Service:* The group can look around its community and pick up projects as part of adding value to their community and offering service to humanity. This will create a sense of fulfilment in them as people who are adding value to the lives of others. The activity could be volunteering at a nearby orphanage or motherless babies' home to help in putting smiles on the faces of the children and improving their lives. Another community service activity could also be community sanitation. Members of the group can pick up a day from time to time to do a cleanup of their surroundings. One good thing about this activity is that other members of the community will, out of joy, come to join them in cleaning.

- *Group Workout:* Exercising is a very important part of a fat girl's life. And it is common to find girls who are too lazy to exercise regularly. A journal group can set aside some days for a group workout. This will serve as motivation for all members of the group. Exercising as a group is a lot easier than personal exercise, because at the point when you are about to give up, seeing others doing it will motivate you to continue.

If you do not find any journal group around you, you can go ahead and create one. Get in touch with one or two fat girls around you, give them the idea, and you can get others to join the group.

A Fat Girl Also Gets Tired: Ways to Have Fun, Recharge Yourself and Relax Your Body

Just like every normal human being, the fat girl also gets tired. If you have a stressful job coupled with chores at home, you will feel tired at the end of your day. And most times, you are always too busy to pause and take a rest because you are eager to make more money and live an even better and richer life. But then if you stress your body too much, it will react. You will break down, and when you do, you will be forced to take that rest your body has always needed. The wise thing to do will be not to wait until you break down before getting a rest. And you know why? You will never get to that point when you can say that you have made enough money; the more money you make, the more money you hunger to make. That is human.

What Happens When a Fat Girl Gets Tired?

When you get tired but refuse to step aside and take a rest, as I have said, you will break down. But before a total breakdown, there are other effects of not getting rest when you should. When you are tired, you are more vulnerable to irritations and anxieties; little things will provoke you, things that you would have ignored on a good day. You will snap at people for little or no reasons, you will not be able to fulfil your daily goals, and you will not be motivated to do anything peacefully. And you will not be the only one involved in this, people around you will also be at the receiving end of your tiredness. They will also get mad at you for giving them attitude, and you can even spoil a good relationship at the delicate moment of tiredness.

What to Do When You Get Tired

Rest: That sounds easy, right? But how often do you have rest? How often do you set aside everything and get some well-needed rest? Look, whether you are working for yourself or someone else, if you drop dead today, no great change will take place. Your boss will hire someone else, or members of your family will take over your business. So, in the end, nothing is worth dying for. I repeat, when you get tired, take a rest.

And before I continue, I want to note that it is common to see ladies involve themselves in self-induced stress in a bid to please the men in their lives. For instance, a girl who is hoping that her boyfriend marries her may feel the need to present herself as one who never gets tired in a bid to convince the young man that she will make a good wife. This sounds pathetic, but it is true - pathetically so. There is no need for this because if you do the basic things you are supposed to do as a responsible adult, a reasonable man who loves you will not even be on the lookout for all of that. Whatever show you put up before marriage should be maintained in marriage or there will be trouble. Do I still need to remind you that if you drop dead today, your dear boyfriend or husband will move on with his life, and most likely with another woman? So, never project yourself as one who never gets tired. When you get tired, please take some rest.

4 Ways to Relax and Have Fun

You probably know some of these already, but it is okay if you do not. We are talking about ways to relax and have fun when you get tired, and we have some of them below.

Have a Me Time: One good way to relax after having a stressful day is to sneak away from everything and everybody and have some quiet time alone. These days, it is difficult for people to truly have rest because even when they step aside to have rest, they will still pick up their phones and jump from one corner to the other on the internet, especially social media. So, while it seems like they are taking a rest, their brain is still actively engaged in what could cause them stress. But a complete rest will require staying away from everything. It could be fun, you know.

Take a Walk: Taking a walk for relaxation feels like you are literally walking away from your burdens. This is usually better in the evening when the sun is down, and you can enjoy the cool breeze of nature.

Go out with Friends: Going out with friends is also a way of relaxing. You may not be resting your body because of the activities you may get involved with, but you will get distracted from work and stress, including mental stress.

Watch a Movie: When you see a movie, you are relaxing your mind from over thinking and analysis of problems of life. You just relax and watch as fiction plays on screen. When picking a movie for relaxation, it is preferable that you pick a comedy, so you can laugh and relax your muscles. Going for tragic or horror movies may not be good for relaxation because they are usually very intense. You can watch the movie at home or the cinema, alone or in the company of friends.

Now that we have seen some ways to rest when we get tired; let's look at some benefits of these activities regarding health and social life.

Health and Social Implications of Rest and Relaxation

When you have rest, you will be able to function better. Your body will not wear out sooner than supposed to, and your mind will be stable. Having enough rest gives you a clearer mind to tackle issues in your life. If you are tired and still insist on not taking a rest, some solutions to simple problems you could have easily solved will elude you. But go back to that same problem after you have been well rested, and you will find out that, even if you do not have an immediate solution, you will at least have a clearer picture of what the problem is all about.

Having rest can keep your body strong from the attack of sickness. We fall sick most times because our body is too weak to resist or withstand the causes of the sickness. Resting may not be the ultimate prevention for sickness and disease, but it at least reduces the rate at which you fall sick. Your mental health is also in consideration here; having enough rest helps you have a more stable mind.

The benefits of having enough rest have on your social life cannot be overemphasized. You probably would not have a social life if you do not time to relax. First, you will be at peace with yourself and will have little or no anxiety. When this is the case, it will rub off on the people around you. People will want to be around you because you will be cheerful.

In all this, you can see that achieving the fat girl's confidence takes so much work, much more on the inside than on the outside. I encourage you to take all aspects of your life seriously. And I celebrate with you as you achieve your fat girl's confidence.

Conclusion

With all of this, you can see that a fat girl's confidence is an all-around process. The confident fat girl is physically fit (you judge your very own fit), mentally and spiritually sound, and socially vibrant. She is confident in everything she does. As you come to the end of this session, do not close this book and forget all that you have learned. Refer to it from time to time to remind yourself what you may be forgetting. And never forget that you are beautiful just the way you are.

Please feel free to share your stories of being forced into shame or the bullying process that you have been through; I would like to include your voices as I take my journey into find self-actualization. One thing for sure is that you all must know we share the same connections and flaws. You are amongst the confident, high self-esteem hierarchy of beauty queens. Award yourself such because you have earned it.

A Fat Girl's Confidence Pledge

I pledge to be ______________________________. I love myself_____________________. My ___________________ cares for me and I know this because ___________________. I can call ____________________ when I need help. I pledge to never let my ____________________ get me down in my feelings. I will not continue to _________________. I have learned that ______________________________ is the old me and I no longer know that person. I am now a __________________________. I pledge to love myself, boldly and unapologetically. I am confident that I can master all my short-term goals of ______________ within five years. I will master my long-term goals within the next ten years.

Yours truly, __________________

A bold, beautiful, confident fat girl with a dream.

Please come back and review this pledge as the years go by. Keep it in a safe place. If your goals are to lose weight, come back and look at your fat girl's confidence pledge as you compare and contrast your growth. We will all grow together.

A Fat Girl's Confidence Pledge (Example)

I pledge to be **me**. I love myself **excessively**. My **family** cares for me and I know this because they **support me.** I can call **on God** when I need help. I pledge to never let my **negative thoughts** get me down in my feelings. I will not continue to **procrastinate through emotion.** I have learned that **keeping my feelings bottled-up** is the old me and I no longer know that person. I am now a **successful woman because I have started to love me.** I pledge to love myself, boldly and unapologetically. I am confident that I can master all my short-term goals of **building my self-esteem, self-image and inner beauty** within five years. I will master my long-term goals within the next ten years.

Yours truly, **Patrice Shavone Brown.**

A bold, beautiful, confident fat girl with a dream.

www.ingramcontent.com/pod-product-compliance
Lightning Source LLC
LaVergne TN
LVHW020647100826
845148LV00012B/2370

* 9 7 8 1 7 3 2 8 8 1 8 2 2 *